Date Due

JY 03 '01			

BRODART, CO.   Cat. No. 23-233-003   Printed in U.S.A.

KEN
GRIFFEY
JUNIOR

THE ACHIEVERS

KEN GRIFFEY JUNIOR

ALL-AROUND ALL-STAR

Barbara Kramer

Lerner Publications Company • Minneapolis

For Terry, who encouraged me to follow my dream

Information for this book was obtained from the following sources:
Boys' Life, Chicago Tribune, Cincinnati Post, Daily Herald, Ebony, Esquire, Jet, Los Angeles Times, Minneapolis Star Tribune, New York Times, Newsweek, People, Pittsburgh Press, Sacramento Union, Seattle Mariners Baseball Team, *Seattle Times, Sport, Sports Card Trader, Sports Cards, Sports Illustrated, Portland Oregonian, The Sporting News, This Year in Baseball 1991* by Bob Carroll, *USA Today, USA Today Baseball Weekly, Washington Post.*

This book is available in two editions:
Library binding by Lerner Publications Company
Soft cover by First Avenue Editions
241 First Avenue North, Minneapolis, Minnesota 55401

International Standard Book Number: 0-8225-2887-8 (lib. bdg.)
International Standard Book Number: 0-8225-9729-2 (pbk.)

LIBRARY OF CONGRESS CATALOGING-IN-PUBLICATION DATA

Kramer, Barbara.
    Ken Griffey Junior : all-around all-star / Barbara Kramer.
        p.   cm. — (The Achievers)
    Summary: A biography of Ken Griffey, Jr., who joined the Seattle Mariners as the youngest player in the American League in 1989.
    ISBN 0-8225-2887-8
    1. Griffey, Ken, Jr. — Juvenile literature. 2. Baseball players — United States — Biography — Juvenile literature. [1. Griffey, Ken, Jr. 2. Baseball players. 3. Afro-Americans — Biography.]
I. Title. II. Series.
GV865.G69K73   1996
796.357'092—dc20
[B]   96–3860

Manufactured in the United States of America
1 2 3 4 5 6 – JR – 01 00 99 98 97 96

Contents

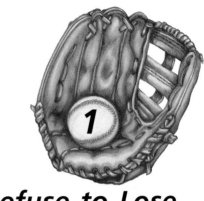

Refuse to Lose

Ken Griffey Jr. strolled out to home plate. He took a few practice swings and then stepped into the batter's box. His face showed no signs of tension even though this was the biggest game of his career.

For the first time, the Seattle Mariners were in the postseason playoffs. They were playing the Yankees in an American League divisional playoff series. Both teams had won two games in the best-of-five-games series. The winner of this game would go to the American League Championship Series with a chance to play in the World Series.

More than 57,000 baseball fans had jammed into the Kingdome to support their hometown team. So far, they hadn't had much to cheer. In the bottom of the eighth inning, the Yankees led, 4–2. Seattle had one out and no runners on base. If the

Mariners were to keep their playoff hopes alive, they needed a big play.

Ken Griffey Jr.—Junior as he is called—is an all-around player. That means he plays well on both offense and defense. "He can beat you with his glove, with his arm, with his speed, and with his bat," former Mariners manager Jim Lefebvre once said.

Mariners fans were counting on Junior's bat to get their team back in the game. Yankees starting pitcher David Cone threw Junior a pitch. Junior hit the ball high and deep into the outfield. It disappeared into the stands—a home run!

The crowd went wild. Fans sprang to their feet, shouting and waving signs that read "Refuse to Lose." "Refuse to Lose" was a Mariners' slogan. The fans created it to encourage their team after the Mariners lost the first two games of the series.

The Mariners still needed a run to tie the game. After Edgar Martinez grounded out, the Mariners were down to their final out. They loaded the bases with two walks and another hit off Cone. Pinch hitter Doug Strange was next to bat. With the count at 3–2, Cone threw a forkball that went into the dirt to walk in the tying run. Yankees manager Buck Showalter brought in rookie relief pitcher Mariano Rivera. He threw just three pitches to get the third out.

Junior watches a home run ball fly out of the Kingdome.

Neither team scored in the ninth, so the game went into extra innings. The Yankees scored a run in the top of the 11th. Once again, the Mariners were in a must-score situation.

Second baseman Joey Cora led off in the bottom half of the 11th inning. He bunted and was safe at first. Then Junior ripped a single to centerfield. Cora raced to third base on Junior's hit. Junior stopped at first. The Mariners could tie the game with a single. The winning run—Junior—was on first, and there were no outs.

Edgar Martinez was up to bat. On the second pitch, he pulled the ball into the leftfield corner for a double. Cora scored easily to tie the game again, but Junior was not going to settle for a tie. Running faster than he had ever run, he raced for third. The third base coach waved his arms, signaling Junior to keep going. Junior charged down the third base line. He slid across home plate to score the winning run.

Fireworks exploded overhead. Junior's teammates burst out of the dugout to congratulate him. They jumped on top of him. The whole team collapsed in a heap. Junior looked out from the bottom of the stack. His grin seemed to stretch all the way across his face. He had refused to lose. The Mariners had won their first playoff series!

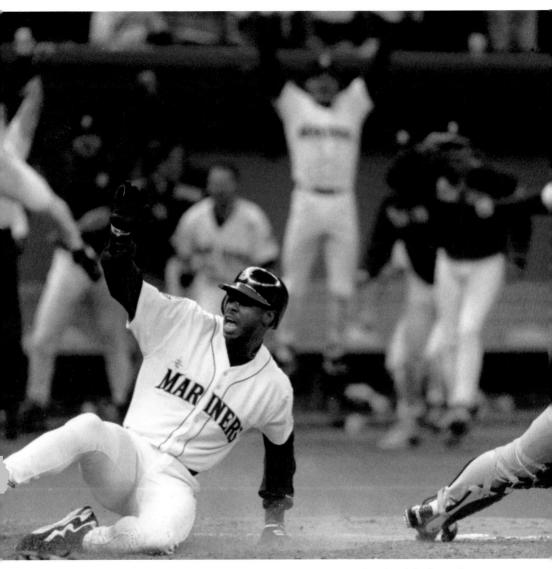

Junior slides home to score the winning run in the Mariners'
playoff game against the New York Yankees.

Ken Griffey often took his two sons, Craig in the back and Junior on the right, to the Cincinnati stadium.

A Natural

Some people say Ken Griffey Jr. was born to play baseball. He makes the game look so easy. At least part of the reason that baseball seems natural for him is because he grew up around the game.

Ken Griffey Jr. was born on November 21, 1969, in Donora, Pennsylvania. He was named George Kenneth Griffey, same as his dad. Both Griffeys go by their middle names. Junior was the first child born to Ken and Alberta Griffey. They had another son, Craig, in 1971. Their daughter, Lathesia, was born two years later.

Alberta and Ken had gotten together when they were in high school. They had shared an interest in sports. Ken starred in baseball, track, and football at Donora High School. Alberta played volleyball and basketball. They were married shortly after they graduated.

The Cincinnati Reds picked Ken in the 29th round of the baseball draft. He went directly from high school into their minor league system. Each major league team has at least four minor league teams. In the minor leagues, players work on their skills and try to advance to the major league team.

Minor league players often don't earn much money. During the off-seasons, Ken took odd jobs to support his family. The family sometimes relied on welfare checks when Ken couldn't find work. The Griffeys had more money when Ken made the Cincinnati Reds' major league team in 1973.

The players' kids were welcome at Riverfront Stadium, the Reds' home field. Before the games, Ken would pitch to Junior. "I've been hitting off him since I was real little," Junior says. "I hated for him to throw it underhand, so he pitched over-hand to me." Junior liked to wear his dad's hat, but it was too large. He had to wear the hat backward to keep it from sliding over his eyes.

It was an exciting time to be part of the Reds' organization. Many great players, such as Pete Rose, Tony Perez, and Johnny Bench played on that team. Ken played right field for the "Big Red Machine," which became the team's nickname since it had so many powerful hitters. The Reds won the World Series two years in a row—in 1975 and 1976.

Junior, center, and his brother Craig loved to go to work
with their dad at the ballpark.

Junior says most of the time he didn't think of his dad as being a baseball star. At home, he was simply "Dad." He played catch in the backyard with Junior or challenged him in games of one-on-one basketball.

Sometimes Junior felt extremely proud to say his dad was a major league baseball player. One of those times was July 8, 1980. Ken was playing in the All-Star Game at Dodger Stadium in Los Angeles, California. Junior sprawled in front of the television set to watch the game. He saw his dad hit a home run in the fifth inning. Ken was named the MVP (most valuable player) for the game. That was a night 10-year-old Junior never forgot.

Junior's dad hit 60 home runs during the first nine years that he played with the Cincinnati Reds.

After Junior's dad hit this home run in the fifth inning of the 1980 All-Star Game, he was named the Most Valuable Player of the game.

When Junior's dad was 31, he was traded to the Yankees. That meant Junior's mom, Alberta, had to manage the family in Cincinnati while his dad played in New York.

Life changed for the Griffeys in 1981. Ken was traded to the New York Yankees. During the baseball season, Ken went to New York and the rest of the family stayed in Cincinnati. Junior went to school and played Little League baseball in Cincinnati.

Because Ken was away much of the time, it was up to Alberta Griffey to make sure that Junior behaved. When she thought Junior needed his father's guidance, she put him on an airplane headed for New York City.

The first time that happened, Junior thought he was in trouble with his dad. Instead, Ken took him to the ballpark for batting practice. After that, Junior looked forward to his trips to the city. Ken says he thinks his son misbehaved a few times on purpose, just so his mother would send him to New York City.

Spring training was different. Then the whole family got to be together in Florida. The children had a special tutor for their schooling. Every day, Junior would go to the ballpark. He would shag baseballs for his dad and the other players.

Like his dad, Junior throws and bats left-handed. Junior says he learned to hit left-handed pitchers by having his dad pitch to him. Ken threw his son fastballs, curveballs, changeups, even sliders. Junior could hit them all. "After age 12, I couldn't strike him out," Ken remembers.

As a nine-year-old, Junior loved to play Little League baseball. He was nervous when his dad watched him.

Ken rarely got to see Junior play in a game. During the baseball season, he and Junior played ball in different parts of the country. Occasionally, when Ken had a day off, he would go to one of Junior's games. On those days, Junior didn't play well.

By the time Junior was 14 years old, major league scouts were already interested in him. Playing in front of baseball scouts never seemed to bother Junior, but having his dad there made him nervous. "When he was there, it was the only time I thought I had to impress somebody," Junior said. "He'd say he was the one guy I didn't have to impress."

Junior had the ability to be a good student, but he didn't always work at it. He would let his studies slide and then try to salvage a poor grade by doing well on a big test. His last-minute efforts sometimes failed.

Poor grades kept Junior from playing baseball during his first year at Cincinnati's Archbishop Moeller High School. The next year, he decided to go to spring training with his dad rather than play baseball for the high school team. In his junior year, he began to play high school baseball. Despite the late start, Junior managed to set school records for the number of career home runs (20) and for the most home runs hit in a single season (11). Although he did some pitching for the team, he preferred to play in the outfield.

Junior played wide receiver for Moeller High's football team (right), but baseball (above) was his first love.

Junior also played baseball for the Connie Mack League, a league for older teenagers. He began playing in that league when he was 16 years old, although most of his teammates were 18.

Junior's speed made him an excellent wide receiver on Moeller High School's football team. He was offered a scholarship to play football at Oklahoma. He turned down Oklahoma when the Mariners picked him first in the 1987 baseball draft. They chose him before 1,263 other players. The draft came a few days before Junior graduated from high school. He was 17 years old.

Junior began his professional baseball career on a Class A
team in Bellingham, Washington.

24

Growing Up in the Minors

The Mariners made their first appearance in the American League in 1977. They had never had a winning season. Junior wasn't concerned about the team's record. "I don't follow baseball like a fan does, so it didn't matter to me," he said. "What mattered is that my dad said they had outfield openings and it was a good opportunity."

Junior spent his first year with the Mariners in Bellingham, Washington, playing for a Class A team. The minor league teams are divided into levels: Class AAA (the highest level), Class AA, Class A, and the rookie league. In his first week as a professional, Junior hit three home runs and drove in eight runs.

Off the field, things didn't go as well. The life of a minor league player isn't easy. Instead of the chartered flights that Ken enjoyed in the majors, Junior's team traveled to games in a 1958 school bus. The bus had no restrooms and sometimes the trips were 10 hours long. The team's bus driver had two teenage sons who didn't get along with Junior. Junior said one of the boys called him a "nigger." The other one threatened to come after Junior with a gun. "Growing up back home, I never had to deal with anything like that," Junior later said. Adding to Junior's problems was the fact that he was away from home for the first time. He was homesick.

His parents did what they could to support him long distance. Junior called his mother every night. He always reversed the charges. Once, he ran up his mom's monthly phone bill to $600. He called his dad too. "He tells me to call him whenever I want," Junior explained to a reporter.

Junior's problems off the field affected his playing. His batting average fell to .230. He felt discouraged. "When I can't hit, that's when I want to quit," he said. Then he was benched for violating the team's curfew. Alberta Griffey took action. She flew to Bellingham to talk to her son. "I knew he needed some sympathy," she said. "But I got mad and told him to concentrate on his career."

At first, Junior was angry with his mother. He didn't call her for four days. But Junior was not the type of person who could stay angry for long. He went back to calling his mother nightly. He also began hitting the ball again.

Before he was drafted, Junior visited in the Atlanta dugout with his dad, who had joined the Braves in 1987.

Junior's Class A Bellingham team played its home games at Joe Martin Field.

He ended the season with a .313 batting average, including 14 home runs and 40 RBIs (runs batted in). He was also named to the all-league outfield.

The Bellingham club had a short season. When it ended, Junior was sent to the Instructional League in Arizona. Only a few minor league players were selected to receive additional training in the Instructional League. It was an honor for Junior to be chosen, but it meant another month away from his family.

When he finally got back to Cincinnati, he found living at home again was difficult after being on his own. Junior and his dad often argued about things like curfews and being responsible. "It seemed like everyone was yelling at me in baseball, then I came home and everyone was yelling at me there," Junior remembers. He became depressed.

By January, Junior had reached his lowest point. He tried to kill himself by swallowing a large bottle of aspirins. His girlfriend's mother rushed him to a hospital where doctors pumped his stomach.

"It was a dumb thing to do," Junior later said. He urged other teenagers to find better ways to deal with their problems. "Don't ever try to commit suicide," he said. "I am living proof how stupid that is."

Junior and his dad were able to work through their differences. "Maybe it was a case of me growing up," Junior said. When spring training rolled around, they were both ready to play ball.

Junior began the 1988 season in San Bernardino,

California, where he played for the Spirit, a Class A team. He got off to a great start, hitting over .500 in the first two weeks.

Before the games, Junior and some of his teammates liked to loosen up by singing rap music. Junior even looked like a rap musician. He wore gold necklaces, a gold earring, and turned his hat backwards.

Junior's baseball skills and his cheerful outlook made him a crowd favorite. When he stepped up to bat, the announcer would say, "What time is it?" The crowd would shout, "It's Griffey time!"

Ken was playing for the Atlanta Braves that season. In April, after an afternoon game with the Dodgers in Los Angeles, he rented a car and drove 90 miles to watch his son play.

Although Junior was happy to see his dad, he was also nervous. He always had trouble getting hits when his dad was in the stands. In his first at bat that day, Junior bunted for a base hit. "I was going to get at least one hit, even if he [Dad] gets on me about it," Junior joked.

In the bottom half of the eighth inning, Junior hit a shot deep into left field. The ball fell behind a group of trees more than 400 feet away. Junior laughed to himself as he ran the bases. Finally he had launched one out of the ballpark with his dad watching.

On June 9, Junior injured his back. He was on the disabled list until August 15. However, because he had played so well before the injury, he was moved up to the Mariners' Class AA team in Vermont. He finished the season there.

The Kid

Almost everyone connected with the Mariners' organization expected Junior to spend the 1989 season in Calgary, playing for the Mariners' Class AAA team. But Junior went all out in spring training. He hit .359 in 26 exhibition games. He had 33 hits and 21 RBIs—both spring training records for Seattle.

On March 29, the Mariners manager, Jim Lefebvre, called Junior aside. "Congratulations!" he said. "You're my centerfielder." Junior was 19 years old—the youngest player in the American League.

The next day, Junior's dad signed a one-year contract with the Cincinnati Reds. That day, the Griffeys became the first father and son to play in the majors at the same time.

On opening day of the regular season, Junior doubled in his first at bat. A week later, in the Mariners' first home game, he hit a home run on the first pitch of his first at bat.

Junior's dad rejoined the Cincinnati Reds in 1989.

Then he fell into a batting slump. By April 22, his batting average was a dismal .189. It was time to find out if Junior was really ready to play major league baseball. Could he work his way out of a batting slump or would he be sent to a Class AAA team?

Junior answered that question in his next five games. He got a hit in 13 of his next 16 at bats, raising his average to .333. He tied a Mariners record for consecutive hits (8) and was named American League Player of the Week for April 24–30.

He was also leading the team in standing ovations. Fans applauded his feats on the field, but they also liked his personality. He always seemed to be smiling and having fun. Junior was like a big kid playing a man's game. In fact, that's what people started calling him—"The Kid."

Junior seemed a sure bet for Rookie of the Year, but those hopes ended when he was injured in an accident off the field. According to newspaper accounts, Junior slipped as he was coming out of the shower in his hotel room after a game in Chicago. He used his hand to catch himself and broke a bone in the little finger of his right hand.

He was on the disabled list from July 24 to August 20. When he began playing again, he tried to make up for lost time.

Junior was younger than his Mariners teammates.

Junior had set a goal for himself to hit 20 home runs that season. He had 13 before he was injured. "I was worrying about hitting the ball 700 feet," he said. During September and October, he batted just .181. His average for the season dropped to .264. Junior finished the season with 61 RBIs, 61 runs, 16 stolen bases, and 16 home runs.

Junior thanks his mom, Alberta, for her support.

In the meantime, his personal life was improving. A young woman named Melissa had the courage to ask Junior to dance one night. They were at an under-21 club that they both liked because alcohol was not served there. Melissa didn't know much about baseball. She and Junior did share other interests, though, such as fishing, jet skiing, and having paint gun fights with their friends. They began dating.

In the 1990 season, Junior became the first Mariner to start in an All-Star game. In August, he celebrated another first when the Mariners acquired Ken from the Cincinnati Reds. Junior and his dad became the first father and son to play for the same major league team at the same time.

On August 31, Ken joined his son in the Mariners' outfield. At 6 feet 3 inches, 205 pounds, Junior was taller and slimmer than his dad, who measured in at 6 feet, 210 pounds. Junior followed his dad in the batting lineup. In their first game as teammates, they got back-to-back base hits.

Two weeks later, in a game against the Angels at Anaheim Stadium, Ken hit his first home run for the Mariners. As he crossed home plate, he high-fived Junior and joked, "That's the way you do it son."

Then Junior batted. With the count three balls and no strikes, Junior swung and connected for a home run.

Junior and his dad became Mariners teammates in 1990.

Junior high-fives his dad after his father hit a home run.
Then, Junior hit one of his own.

He circled the bases, then ran into the dugout and hugged his dad. "We could've lost all our games the rest of the season and I wouldn't have cared," Junior said. "We were having such a great time playing together, being teammates, playing baseball."

Junior finished the season with 22 home runs and 80 RBIs. He also earned his first Gold Glove Award, for outstanding defensive play.

That year, Junior also became involved with the Seattle chapter of the Make-a-Wish Foundation. The Make-a-Wish foundation grants children with life-threatening illnesses a wish of their choice. Junior became involved with the organization when he agreed to take a child out to dinner. On the way home in a limousine, the child fell asleep on Junior's shoulder. Since then, there have been many other children whose one wish was to meet Junior. He has never turned down a request from the foundation.

Not Good Enough?

Junior got a huge raise at the start of the 1991 season when he signed a two-year contract extension worth $2 million. By midseason, Junior was hitting .280 with 9 home runs and 36 RBIs. Although those weren't bad numbers, Junior still had critics.

Some ballplayers study opposing pitchers. They keep track of the pitcher's strengths and weaknesses in small notebooks. Junior doesn't do that. In batting practice before a game, he likes to wear his hat backwards. He jokes and clowns around with other players, coaches, and reporters. To his critics, these were signs that he wasn't serious about the game.

A columnist for a Seattle newspaper wrote an article criticizing Junior's lack of dedication and focus. He challenged Junior to do better. The reporter wrote that it was time for Junior to decide if he wanted to settle for being good, or if he wanted to push himself to be great. "It was a bad article," Junior later said, "but it came out good. It made me think about the person I want to be and what I can accomplish in this game."

The article was published during the 1991 All-Star Game break. Junior responded by having his best month since he had been in the major leagues. During that July, he batted .434, the highest average in the league. He ended the season with 22 home runs and 100 RBIs. For his offensive efforts, he received a Silver Slugger Award.

That year, for the first time in the team's history, the Mariners had a winning season. Seattle finished fifth in the Western Division with a record of 83 wins and 79 losses.

A third Griffey had signed with the Mariners in 1991. Junior's brother, Craig, had been attending Ohio State University on a football scholarship. In 1991, he decided to switch to baseball. He was drafted by the Mariners and spent his first season playing on their Rookie League team in Tempe, Arizona.

But the Mariners lost a Griffey at the end of the season. During spring training Ken had hurt his neck in a car accident in Phoenix, Arizona. Because of his injury, he wasn't able to play much in the 1991 season. At the end of the season, he retired from baseball. He stayed with the Mariners' organization, however, as a hitting instructor.

In 1992, Junior was again chosen to start in the All-Star Game. He hit a single, a double, and a home run as the American League defeated the National League, 13–6. Junior won the MVP award— another entry for the history books. Junior and Ken became the first father and son to hit a home run in and be named MVP of an All-Star Game. For Ken, that honor had come 12 years earlier.

Junior and his dad were teammates until Ken retired in 1991.

Junior's acrobatic catches in centerfield have earned him defensive honors. He holds the American League record for most outfield plays without an error.

Junior didn't become just the All-Star Game MVP that year. He also became a husband when he married his girlfriend, Melissa. They had known each other for almost three years, but Junior's popularity still amazed Melissa. "It's crazy out there," she once told a reporter. "When we go out together, which we rarely do, I'll say to Ken, 'Why are they acting that way?' All he says is, 'I may be Ken to you, but I'm Junior to them.'"

Hitting home runs is what Junior does best on offense.

During the off-season, there were rumors that Junior was becoming discouraged with the Mariners' losing ways. After a winning season in 1991, they had finished the 1992 season with their worst record since Junior had joined the team. Junior remained committed to Seattle, however, and in 1993 he signed a $24-million, four-year contract.

In his first four seasons in the majors, Junior averaged 22 home runs a season. In 1993, he more than doubled that figure with 45 homers. Eight of those home runs came in one incredible week in July. From July 20 to 28, Junior hit a home run in eight consecutive games. He tied the major league record for the most consecutive home runs in a season. Only two other players had ever done that —the Pirates' Dale Long in 1956 and the Yankees' Don Mattingly in 1987.

On July 29, fans gathered in the Kingdome for a game against the Minnesota Twins. They were hoping to see Junior break the record. They cheered when Junior hit a single and a double in his first four at bats. His last at bat came in the seventh inning when he popped up a curveball to end the streak. Mariners pitcher Erik Hanson later commented about the way fans had cheered for Junior that night. "If he had hit a home run his last at bat, the roof would have come off, and we'd have an outdoor stadium," Hanson said.

Junior's dad was with him on July 29, 1993, when his consecutive-game home run streak ended.

For the second time, the Mariners had a winning season with 82 wins and 80 losses. Junior led the team in every offensive category. He was just as impressive on defense. He set an American League record, making 573 outfield plays without an error. He earned his fourth consecutive Gold Glove Award and his second Silver Slugger Award.

A wild pitch brings Junior sliding home from third base.

After Junior's successful year, reporters and other players began asking Junior when he was going to ask the Mariners for a better contract. Their questions only angered Junior. He said, "I will never, ever go to the Mariners and ask to redo a contract just because I had a great year. That's what they're paying me for in the first place."

That fall, Junior got a chance to add the word "actor" to his list of accomplishments. He was offered a part in the movie *Little Big League*. He had a small role in the movie about a 12-year-old boy who becomes the owner of the Minnesota Twins.

Junior spent the last part of the off-season getting to know his son. Trey Kenneth Griffey was born in January 1994. Junior and Melissa thought about naming their son George Kenneth Griffey III. Instead, they settled on Trey Kenneth. Trey means three.

The most unusual baby gift they received came from Mariners General Manager Woody Woodward. As a joke, he sent Trey a Mariners' contract dated for the year 2012. Junior, acting as his son's manager, did not return the signed contract. "It wasn't enough money," he joked.

A Bad Time for a Good Year

The 1994 season looked to be an outstanding year for Junior. In May, he broke the record for the number of home runs in the first two months of the season. Mickey Mantle, a slugger for the Yankees, had set the record in 1956 by hitting 20 home runs before June 1. Junior hit his 21st home run on May 23. He was on track to break Roger Maris's 1961 record for the number of home runs in a season (61).

Junior had always been a star, but now he was at the center of the media's attention. Other players were amazed at how well he handled the pressure. "If you saw what he goes through on a daily basis . . . ," explained Junior's friend and teammate, Jay Buhner. "Yet when he steps across the line, he's happy-go-lucky and loves to play the game."

The Mariners tried to take some of the pressure off Junior by scheduling Griffey news conferences before the first game of each series. Then, for the rest of the series, Junior was off-limits to reporters.

But Junior also had to deal with his fans. Junior is willing to sign autographs inside the ballpark and he takes a special interest in kids. Although he could never sign enough autographs to satisfy all his fans, he tries not to turn away any kids. "It tears me up to see one put his head down disappointed," he says.

On the other hand, Junior has seen a dark side to some of his fans. They have scratched Junior's car as he drove away from the ballpark just because he wouldn't stop and give them his autograph. Junior estimates that in 1993 he spent more than $100,000 to repair scratches on his cars, put there by disappointed autograph seekers.

Even worse are the fans who try to scare him. After a game in Tempe, Arizona, a man approached Junior and said in a threatening voice, "Sign this or I could end your career." In June 1994, FBI agents notified Junior that they had intercepted notes threatening Junior's life and the lives of his wife and son. Since then, four of Junior's friends from Cincinnati have moved to Seattle to act as his bodyguards.

In the meantime, Junior continued to hammer out home runs. In 1994, he had 40 homers when the season ended because of a baseball strike.

Fans are eager to talk to Junior and get his autograph.

That figure topped the American League, giving Junior his first home run title. Junior never complained that the players' strike had ruined a good year for him. "I have to do what's best for the players and what's best for the future," he said.

Baseball players everywhere try to model their swings after Junior's classic batting style.

Junior and teammate Jay Buhner provided most of Seattle's scoring punch in the 1995 season.

When the 1995 season began, the players were back on the field. Craig Griffey spent the season playing for the Port City Roosters, a Class AA team in Wilmington, North Carolina. Ken began his first season as coach for the Mariners' Class AAA team in Tacoma, Washington. Junior got off to a slow start in the home run category. He hit number 7 on May 26 in the fifth inning of a home game against the Baltimore Orioles. Two innings later, he crashed into the centerfield wall after making a spectacular catch. His left hand got caught in the fence padding. According to doctors who treated him, his wrist "exploded."

Doctors operated on Junior for three hours. They placed a metal plate and seven screws in his wrist. Junior was expected to spend three months on the disabled list, but he worked hard, exercising his wrist and getting his strength back. He returned to play on August 15, two weeks earlier than predicted. Junior had four hits in his first five games back, including his 1,000th career hit.

Seattle manager Lou Piniella missed having Junior in the Mariners' lineup while Junior's injured arm was healing.

Mariners swarm Junior after he scores the winning run against the Yankees in the fifth game of their series.

That fall, for the first time in the Mariners' history, the team reached the playoffs. Seattle won the best-of-five American League divisional playoff series against the Yankees. Junior set a record in that series when he became the first player to hit five home runs in five games in postseason play.

Despite Junior's efforts, the Cleveland Indians defeated Seattle in the 1995 American League Championship Series and advanced to the World Series.

The Mariners' season ended in the American League Championship Series. Cleveland defeated Seattle to advance to the World Series. Despite the loss, Junior had a reason to celebrate that fall. On October 21, Melissa gave birth to their second child. They named their daughter Taryn. In January 1996, Junior became the highest-paid player in baseball. He signed a four-year contract with Seattle for $8.5 million a year.

As Junior rested his sore hand, he thought back over the Mariners' first playoff season. He was happy to be doing what he does best and having a good time along the way. "When I leave this game, it'll be because I'm not having fun or my skills have diminished," he says. "Otherwise, I'm going to go out and play baseball like it's supposed to be played and enjoy every moment."

Career Highlights

Minor Leagues

Statistics

Year	Team	Games	At Bats	Runs	Hits	Home Runs	Runs Batted In	Stolen Bases	Batting Average
1987	Bellingham	54	182	43	57	14	40	13	.313
1988	San Bernardino	58	219	50	74	11	42	32	.338
1988	Vermont	17	61	10	17	2	10	4	.279
Totals		129	462	103	148	27	96	49	.320

Honors

- Named All-League Outfielder, 1987
- Selected to the California League All-Star Team as an outfielder, 1988

Major Leagues

Statistics

Year	Team	Games	At Bats	Runs	Hits	Home Runs	Runs Batted In	Stolen Bases	Batting Average
1989	Seattle	127	455	61	120	16	61	16	.264
1990	Seattle	155	597	91	179	22	80	16	.300
1991	Seattle	154	548	76	179	22	100	18	.327
1992	Seattle	142	565	83	174	27	103	10	.323
1993	Seattle	156	582	113	180	45	109	17	.308
1994	Seattle	111	433	94	140	40	90	11	.306
1995	Seattle	72	260	52	67	17	42	4	.258
Totals		917	3,440	570	1,039	189	585	92	.302

Honors

- American League All-Star Team, 1990, 1991, 1992, 1993, 1994, 1995*
- Gold Glove Award, 1990, 1991, 1992, 1993, 1994, 1995
- Silver Slugger Award, 1991, 1993, 1994
- Most Valuable Player in the All-Star Game, 1992
- American League Home Run Champion, 1994

*Selected for the team but could not play because of an injury.

ABOUT THE AUTHOR

Barbara Kramer has a Bachelor of Arts degree in English and works as a teacher and freelance writer. She has had a lifelong interest in sports and enjoys writing about real people. She has two grown children and lives with her husband in Cedar Rapids, Iowa.

ACKNOWLEDGMENTS

Photographs are reproduced with the permission of: pp. 1, 2, 57, 62, © John Klein; pp. 6, 9, 11, 58, 59, AP/Wide World Photos; pp. 12, 37, Cincinnati Enquirer/Michael E. Keating; pp. 15, 20, 23, Cincinnati Enquirer; p. 16, The Cincinnati Reds; pp. 17, 18, 27, 40, 45, 46, UPI/Bettmann; p. 22, Coach Mike Cameron/Archbishop Moeller High School; pp. 24, 28, The Bellingham Herald; pp. 32, 36, 42, 47, SportsChrome East/West; p. 34, © ALLSPORT USA/Kirk Schlea; p. 35, SportsChrome East/West, C. Rydlewski; p 39, SportsChrome East/West, Mike Kullen; p. 49, 50, 55, Bettmann; p. 52, SportsChrome East/West, Vincent Manniello; p. 56, SportsChrome East/West, Rob Tringali Jr.; p. 60, © ALLSPORT USA/Stephen Dunn; p. 64, Barbara Kramer.

Front cover photograph by SportsChrome East/West. Back cover photograph by John Klein.

Artwork by John Erste.